What's a FISH?

Anna Kaspar

PowerKiDS press

New York

For my Aunt Fish

Published in 2013 by The Rosen Publishing Group, Inc.
29 East 21st Street, New York, NY 10010

First Edition

Editor: Amelie von Zumbusch
Book Design: Ashley Drago

Photo Credits: Cover © www.iStockphoto.com/Luís Fernando Curci Chavier; p. 5 Paul Souders/ Getty Images; pp. 6, 16 Shutterstock.com; p. 9 © www.iStockphoto.com/Nancy Nehring; pp. 10–11 © www.iStockphoto.com/Rainer von Brandis; p. 12 Medioimages/Photodisc/ Thinkstock; p. 15 © www.iStockphoto.com/Roman Sigaev; p. 19 iStockphoto/Thinkstock; p. 20 Werner Van Steen/Getty Images; p. 23 www.iStockphoto.com/Darren Pearson.

Library of Congress Cataloging-in-Publication Data

Kaspar, Anna.
 What's a fish? / by Anna Kaspar. — 1st ed.
     p. cm. — (All about animals)
 Includes index.
 ISBN 978-1-4488-6135-4 (library binding) — ISBN 978-1-4488-6228-3 (pbk.) —
ISBN 978-1-4488-6229-0 (6-pack)
 1. Fishes—Juvenile literature. I. Title.
 QL617.2.K37 2013
 597—dc23
                                        2011017101

Manufactured in the United States of America

CPSIA Compliance Information: Batch #CS12PK: For Further Information contact Rosen Publishing, New York, New York at 1-800-237-9932

Contents

* * * * * * * * * * * * *

Fish are a type of animal.
Most fish have **fins**.

All fish live in water. Fish are covered in **scales**.

Fish have **gills**. They use their gills to breathe.

Some kinds of fish swim in big groups. These are called **schools**.

Longsnout sea horses live in the Atlantic Ocean. Ocean water is salty.

Carp live in freshwater. This is water that is not salty.

Piranhas live in South American rivers. They are known for their sharp teeth.

Lionfish are poisonous. Their colors scare off animals that want to eat them.

Great white sharks are hunters.
They find their food by its smell.

Sailfish often jump out of the water. They are the world's fastest fish.

WORDS TO KNOW

fin   gills   scales   school

INDEX

WEB SITES

Due to the changing nature of Internet links, PowerKids Press has developed an online list of Web sites related to the subject of this book. This site is updated regularly. Please use this link to access the list: www.powerkidslinks.com/aaa/fish/